9.   Market value

The market value ratios are important both to investors and to the company. It gives an indication to investors of the reputation of a company in financial circles and the length of time it will take for their investment to be recouped. It gives the company's management an idea of what investors and financial experts think of the company's past performance and future prospects. If a firm's liquidity, asset management, debt management and profitability ratios are all good, then its market value ratios and stock price will be high.

Price/earnings

The *price/earnings ratio* shows how long it would take to recover the cost of an investment. It is calculated as follows:

$$\text{price/earnings ratio} = \frac{\text{market price per share}}{\text{earnings per share}}$$

The earnings per share for the year ended 31 December 1987, was £1 and the market value was £10. The price/earnings ratio is:

$$\frac{10}{1} = 10$$

This means that it would take 10 years to cover the current market price of the share.

Usually, the price/earnings ratio of long, well-established and financially-sound companies are high, whereas in weaker ones, as the returns commensurate with the risks are higher, the price-earnings ratio is low.

9. Market value

UNDERSTANDING RATIOS

UNDERSTANDING RATIOS

A PRACTICAL GUIDE FOR BUSINESS, FINANCE AND BANKING

Raghu Palat

KOGAN
PAGE

First published in 1986 as 'The Magic of Ratios' by Ashwin J Shah, Jaico Publishing House, 121
M G Road, Bombay 400 023.

First published in Great Britain in 1989 by
Kogan Page Ltd,
120 Pentonville Rd, London N1 9JN

Printed and bound in Great Britain by Biddles, Guildford & Kings Lynn

British Library Cataloguing in Publication Data
Palat, Raghu R
  Understanding Ratios
  1. Financial management. Ratios
  I. Title
  658.1'51

ISBN 1-85091-937-2

Contents

Introduction

Financial statements can be daunting. Most people find them overwhelming and often frightening, simply because they do not understand them. As a result, they usually look at the net income and, if it has increased, look no further in the firm belief that all is well. It may not be. The company's profitability may have decreased, although the net profit has increased or its liquidity may have declined. The company may be insolvent.

It is in the analysis of financial statements that ratios come into their own. They help:

- to analyse the performance of a company and compare it with that of other similar companies;
- to determine the relative weaknesses and strengths of a company — whether it is profitable, financially sound and whether its condition is improving or deteriorating;
- to fulfil the needs of those in knowing a company's financial position.

Ratios really put figures into perspective. It is difficult to see how a company is doing by looking at a large number of figures. Ratios summarise the figures in a form that is easily understood, interpreted and used.

Ratios express a relationship between one figure and another. It is important that the relationship between the figures is real, otherwise, the result would be meaningless and serve no purpose. For example, a ratio expressing the cost of sales as a percentage of investments is of no consequence as there is no commonality between the figures, whereas a ratio that expresses gross profit as a percentage of sales indicates the mark-up made on the cost of purchases or the margin earned by the company.

To interpret ratios properly, one must ensure that the ratios being measured are consistent and valid. At a time of rising prices, a current ratio wherein inventories are valued under the 'last in first out' method is meaningless. Similarly, in comparing results, if the length of the periods being compared is different or if there is a large non-recurring income or expense, the ratios calculated would be misleading. If ratios are used to evaluate operating performance, extraordinary items should be excluded as they are non-recurring and do not reflect normal performance. In truth, the usefulness of ratios is entirely dependent on their intelligent and skilful interpretation.

It is also important when interpreting ratios, to be aware of the factors that affect the company such as its management policy, the industry, general business conditions and the state of the economy, otherwise, the conclusion arrived at can be incorrect.

Ratios give strong pointers to areas where one should concentrate. They do not necessarily give answers. They show situations and often raise questions. If a ratio has deteriorated between two years, the analyst must delve into the reason for the deterioration. The answers lie behind the ratios. Ratios are only a starting point and whether a ratio is good or bad depends on the company, the industry, the economy and a specific time. At a period of boom, a gross margin of 20 per cent may be low, whereas during a recession it would be high.

Ratios, in short, are simple, but their usefulness is wholly dependent on their logical and intelligent interpretation. In this book we shall show the reader how to do this. We hope it will provide an easily accessible source of instruction for students of business, accounting, finance and banking and also a source of reference for those actually engaged in one of these professions.

PART 1
Using ratios to evaluate companies

1. Basis of Analysis

Data used in the computation of ratios are drawn from the balance sheet and the income statement or the sources and uses of funds settlement. The financial statements of J Smith Ltd, which will be found on pages 17–19, give an indication of their layout. Having procured the financial statements for a period and calculated the ratios, these should be compared with:

- the budgeted or forecast ratios for the period being analysed;
- the corresponding ratio for the preceding and earlier years;
- the corresponding ratio for a similar firm in the same industry and
- the average ratio for other firms in the industry.

This would indicate the company's standing within the group and whether it is doing better or worse than other similar companies. The ratios can point to areas where corrective action needs to be taken. It can be used as an early warning sign in many instances. It is important to remember that for comparative analysis, a peer group (companies similar in business and size) in the same industry should be used, otherwise the conclusions drawn will be incorrect.

It should be remembered while comparing ratios that the higher the volatility among periods, the higher the risk and uncertainty. It is important to look into the company and, if necessary, into the industry and the economy to ascertain the reason for the volatility.

Comparisons between periods and companies would enable the analyst to establish trends. It is those situations wherein the results do not fall in line with the expected pattern that are worrying. If sales of similar companies in the group increase by 10 per cent, whilst that of the company being analysed grow by only 2 per cent, one should be concerned. If the gross margin earned on sales is 20 per cent and in the current period it leaps to 28 per cent, the cause must be investigated. It may be due, for example, to a change in the method of valuation of stocks, or the cost of sales may have been understated.

A series of ratios by themselves are confusing and can make it difficult to interpret the real situation of the company. Ratios should, therefore, be grouped into those classifications that would enable the analyst to interpret and form conclusions on the strength and weaknesses of the company. Bearing this in mind, the ratios detailed in this book have been grouped under the following classifications:

- margins;
- profitability;
- liquidity;
- debt service capacity;
- asset management/efficiency;
- gearing coverage;
- earnings;
- market value.

2. Margins

Margins indicate returns or earnings on sales. They are useful in:

- characterising the cost structures of businesses;
- comparing performance between companies within an industry;
- assessing trends in management performance.

Margins help the analyst to check whether increases on account of inflation are being passed on to customers or being absorbed in part or in full by the firm. This would give an indication of customer demand and sales trends.

Margins show the effect on income of *product mix*. A low margin may be due to a bad product mix. It is, therefore, important for an analyst to examine how events affect margins and find a reason for changes in variables at each and every level. It is usually the case that low-margin businesses which produce a high return on capital are good businesses.

Gross Margins

The *gross margin* is the excess earned (expressed as a percentage) over the *cost of sales*. It shows the mark-up or *value added* over cost. It shows the *profitability* before expenses. The gross margin is arrived at by dividing the result of sales, less the cost of goods sold by sales and expressing it as a percentage of sales.

$$\text{gross margin} = \frac{\text{sales} - \text{cost of goods sold}}{\text{sales}} \times 100$$

An extract of the results of J Smith Ltd was as follows:

	1987 £(000)	1988 £(000)
Sales	800	1,000
Cost of sales	550	700
Gross profit	250	300
Gross margin (%)	31.25	30.00

Although the gross profit has risen by £50,000, the margin has reduced by 1.25 per cent. This may be due to a number of reasons, eg:

- in order to increase sales, the company has consciously reduced margins;
- owing to increased competition, the margins have been reduced to keep sales up;
- the increase in sales has been due to price increases and the company has not been able to pass all of the inflationary increases in the cost of sales to customers;
- the gross margin has reduced due to the mix of sales being bad, ie more lower profit-bearing products being sold.

The analyst should not, therefore, on seeing a fall in the gross margin, assume that the company is becoming less profitable. It could be as a result of a conscious decision to increase sales. Similarly, an increase in gross margins may be due to a price increase and may also show a fall in sales volume. In short, the reasons behind variations in the gross margin should be investigated to arrive at a conclusion on the performance of the company.

Operating margin

The *operating margin* indicates the profitability of a company before the cost of financing and tax and other miscellaneous income. It is arrived at by deducting operating expenses from the gross profit and expressing the result as a percentage of sales.

$$\text{operating margin} = \frac{\text{gross profit} - \text{expenses}}{\text{sales}} = \frac{\text{operating profit}}{\text{sales}}$$

J Smith Ltd is a company that has been trading in chemicals for many years. Its operating results were as follows:

	1987 £(000)	1988 £(000)
Sales	1,000	1,2000
Cost of goods sold	800	960
Gross profit	200	240
Selling, general and adminstration expenses	150	165
Operating profit	50	75
Operating margin (%)	5.00	6.25

The operating margin of J Smith Ltd has increased by 1.25 per cent. This may be on account of operating expenses not having risen in proportion to the company's growth in sales. This is likely as fixed expenses rise more in concert with inflation than due to growth in sales. However, this is only a possibility and may not be the actual reason.

The operating margin indicates the possible reasons for an increase or decrease in profitability and the analyst must ascertain the actual causes.

Breakeven point

The *breakeven point* indicates the number of items that should be sold by a company in order to meet its fixed costs.

In 1988, G Anderson Ltd sold 900 widgets. Its income statement was as follows:

Sales	£18,000
Less: cost of sales	14,400
Gross income	3,600
Less: selling, general and administrative expenses	2,600
Operating income	1,000
Net non-operating income (expenses)	500
Earnings before interest and tax	1,500
Financing costs	900
Earnings before tax	600

The breakeven point would be arrived at as follows:

$$= \frac{\text{selling, general and administrative expenses and financial costs}}{\text{non-operating income}}$$

$$\frac{\text{gross income/number of items sold}}{} $$
$$= \frac{3,000}{4} \qquad = \quad 750 \text{ units}$$

This illustrates that the company would need to sell 750 items before it can make a profit and that every item sold thereafter would bring to the company a profit of £4.

This ratio can also be calculated after deducting selling costs from the gross profit. The figure reached then is divided by the number of items sold. This is a purer measure as sales expenses do vary in accordance with sales.

This is an important measure in examining the relative profitability of products and is crucial in decision-making when considering the alternative of purchasing an item or making it.

It must be remembered that fixed costs do not generally vary with the volume of sales while variable costs do.

Margin before interest

The *margin before interest* is defined as the rate of profit earned on sales prior to the cost of finance. It is arrived at by expressing earnings before interest and tax as a percentage of sales.

$$\frac{\text{earnings before interest and tax}}{\text{sales}}$$

An extract of the income statement of J Johnson Ltd was as follows:

	£(000)
Sales	1,000
Gross income	250
Selling, general and administrative expenses	180
Operating income	70
Other income	10
Earnings before interest and tax	80
Interest expense	20
Pretax income	60

The margin before interest is $\dfrac{80}{1,000} \times 100 = 8$ per cent.

This is a truer measure of profitability than of pre-tax income: the interest charge would vary from one company to another owing to variations in the method of financing.

Pretax margin

The *pretax margin* shows the rate earned on sales after the cost of financing but before tax. This is computed by expressing the pretax income as a percentage of sales. This, in fact, represents the mark-up included in sales to meet all the expenses of the company.

$$\frac{\text{pretax income}}{\text{sales}}$$

The income statement of H Gordon Ltd included the following:

Sales	£12,000
Earnings before interest and tax	1,000
Interest expense	£400
Pretax income	£600

The company has earned a pretax income of $\dfrac{(600 \times 100)}{(12,000)} = 5$ per cent.

Although this ratio indicates the rate earned after all expenses have been met, it does not necessarily lend itself for comparison with other companies because the cost of financing (interest expense) will vary from company to company in the same way as their funding sources.

Net profit margin

The *net profit margin* indicates the rate of earnings a company earns after tax on sales. It shows the margin on sales that is potentially available for distribution to the shareholders.

$$\text{net profit margin} = \frac{\text{net income after tax}}{\text{sales}} \times 100\%$$

An extract of the income statement of Nonsuch Ltd was as follows:

	£(000)
Sales	1,000
Net income before tax	180
Taxation	90
Net income	90

The net profit margin earned by Nonsuch Ltd is:

$$\frac{90,000}{1,000,000} \times 100 = 9 \text{ per cent.}$$

This ratio shows that the earnings available to shareholders were 9 per cent of sales. This margin enables a company to measure the earnings available to shareholders on increases in sales.

Summary

It should be remembered that low margins are not necessarily bad. There are many large companies that cut prices to be more competitive and thereby increase sales. Businesses with very high sales usually have low margins.

Margins may change due to changes in sales policies, sales price increases, cost increases and product mix changes. At all stages prior to forming an opinion on the operating performance of the company, the reasons for the change should be ascertained.

Margins, therefore, assist the analyst making a realistic analysis of a company's performance to examine cost structures, profitability and the ability of a company to effectively pass on cost increases to consumers.

3. Profitability

Profitability ratios indicate a company's profitability compared to that of other companies within the industry, in relation to previous years and provide a measure of the management's effectiveness as shown by returns generated through sales and investments.

These ratios must be considered in relation to rates of inflation and the cost of capital and borrowings.

Trends in ratios should be evaluated as possible indications of future development.

Because large variations in asset and liability figures during the year can distort the ratios quite materially, the ratios should be calculated on average assets or liabilities. The logic of this is evident when one considers that the income earned is an average figure earned over the whole year and not an amount earned on a particular date.

Return on total assets

The *return on total assets* (ROA) allows an analyst to examine whether:

- the margin on sales earned is reasonable;
- the assets of the company are adequately and effectively used;
- the interest payments made by the company are too high.

This, as a measure, should be used to compare performance between companies within an industry and with previous years. This is computed in the following manner.

$$\text{ROA} = \frac{\text{net income after tax}}{\text{average total assets}}$$

The financial statements of H Gordon Ltd include the following figures:

	1987 £(000)	1988 £(000)
Net income after tax	150	200
Total assets	4,000	6,000

The return on total assets in 1988 is:

$$\frac{200}{0.5 \times (4,000 + 6,000)} \times 100 = 4 \text{ per cent.}$$

The analyst must compare this return with that earned by other similar companies to determine whether the return is reasonable.

Return on common equity

The *return on common equity* (ROE) measures the rate of return on stock-holders' investment. It enables an individual to check whether the return made on an investment is better than other alternatives available. This is calculated by expressing (as a percentage of shareholders' funds), net profit after tax, less dividend on preference stock and minority interest.

$$ROE = \frac{\text{net income after tax} - \text{minority interest} - \text{dividend on preference stock}}{\text{average shareholder's equity}}$$

An extract of the financial statements of H Gordon Ltd reads:

	1987 £(000)	1988 £(000)
Net profit after tax	90	108
Minority interest	9	18
	81	90
Preference dividend	20	20
	61	70

Shareholders' equity is 1,000 (1987) and 1,100 (1988) (including reserves and retained earnings).

The return equity is:

$$\frac{70}{\frac{1}{2} \times (1,000 + 1,100)} = 6.67 \times 100 \text{ per cent.}$$

If alternative investments are available that yield a return in excess of this and carry a higher risk, this would indicate that the company's profitability is low.

Pre-interest return on assets

The *pre-interest return on assets* is a purer measure of profitability in relation to assets because, as a result of interest and tax levied, the net income after tax does not reflect operating figures correctly. This is especially true as interest rates and tax rates may change independently of operating performance. This ratio is used for decisions on pricing and is computed as:

$$\text{pre-interest return on assets} = \frac{\text{earnings before interest and tax}}{\text{average total assets}}$$

The financial statements of F Dixon Ltd included the following

	1987 £(000)	1988 £(000)
Earnings before interest and tax	1,200	1,500
Total assets	10,000	14,000

The pre-interest return on assets in 1985 is:

$$\frac{1,500}{0.5 \times (10,000 + 14,000)} \times 100 = 12.5 \text{ per cent.}$$

The above return should be measured against the return earned by other similar companies to establish whether in fact the return is high or low.

Pre-interest after tax return of assets

This ratio measures management's performance in using assets independent of the financing of those assets. However, it includes tax expense on the argument that tax is a charge on profits. Interest is not considered as it is a payment to a furnisher of capital.

The ratio is computed as:

---

pre-interest after tax return on assets

$$= \frac{\text{net income after tax plus interest expense net of income tax saving}}{\text{average total assets}}$$

A portion of the financial statements of H Gordon Ltd is shown below:

	1987 £(000)	1988 £(000)
Earnings before interest and tax	1,000	1,500
Interest expense	400	500
Pretax income	600	1,000
Tax @ 40%	240	400
Net income	360	600
Total assets	9,000	11,000

Pretax interest after tax (ROA)

$$= \frac{600 + \dfrac{500 \times 40}{100}}{0.5\ (9,000 \times 11,000)} \times 100 \text{ per cent} = 8.0 \text{ per cent.}$$

This ratio indicates that H Gordon Ltd earns a return on assets prior to the cost of financing of 8.0 per cent and in comparing the return earned by the company with that of other similar companies, an analyst can determine whether:

• the assets have been effectively used;
• the return is adequate (considering the size and nature of the company).

Return on total invested capital

The *return on total invested capital* enables a shareholder or an analyst to examine whether the return earned is in excess of that which can be earned elsewhere. Invested capital includes all liabilities that have a cost associated with them and usually includes notes payable, short-term debts, long-term debts, lease obligations, subordinated long-term debts, stockholders' equity and minority interest. This return is calculated as follows:

---

return on total invested capital

$$= \frac{\text{earnings before interest and tax}}{\text{average total invested capital}}$$

The return on capital must, at a minimum, exceed the prevailing rates of interest and the weighted average cost of borrowings. This ratio is an important comparison to the cost of a company's capital.

The earnings before interest and tax of N Neville Ltd was £550,000. Its total invested capital at the end of its financial years ended 31 December 1986 and 31 December 1987 were as follows:

	1986 £(000)	1987 £(000)
Short-term notes payable	50	40
Long-term notes payable	150	110
Term loan	2,220	2,100
Debentures	400	400
Shareholders' equity	350	400
Total invested capital	3,150	3,050

The return on invested capital is:

$$\frac{550}{0.5 \times (3,250 + 3,050)} \times 100 = 16.1 \text{ per cent.}$$

The return earned is 16.1%. If the prevailing rate of interest is higher, ie if money can be invested at a rate that exceeds 16.1 per cent, then the investment in the comapny may be considered inadequate.

After-tax return on average net worth

The *after-tax return on average net worth* measures the effect of financial gearing. A high gearing, due to the tax deductibility of interest, in a good year, helps a company to earn high returns. The return is a very important measure of a management performance since it reflects the company's return to its owners. It should, however, be remembered that excessive gearing can produce high risks.

The return is calculated by deducting the tax from the profits and adjusting this figure for extraordinary items and minority interest in net income and dividing by average net worth for the two years.

This ratio is calculated as:

after-tax return on average net worth

$$= \frac{\text{net income–extraordinary items–minority interest in net income}}{\text{average net worth}}$$

The net income for the year ending 31 December 1988, available to the shareholders of P Rogers Ltd was £105,000. Its average net worth in 1988 was 1,010. The after-tax return earned by P Rogers Ltd in 1988 would be:

$$\frac{105}{1,050} \times 100 = 10 \text{ per cent.}$$

This is the return that a shareholder is interested in as it shows the return that he actually earns on the nominal value of the investment. The investor will, of course, also be interested in the return on the amount paid for the investment (ie share price at the time of purchase).

Summary

As the major aim of a commercial enterprise is profit, the profitability ratios are among the more important group of ratios and must always be examined in depth. All changes in these ratios must be looked into as these can indicate the long-term results of the company.

However, at this juncture, it should be remembered that in comparing profitability, a company with higher profitability ratios is not necessarily better. Companies do, in order to increase sales and profits in actual money terms, trade or sell their goods at lower prices.

J SMITH LTD
BALANCE SHEET AS ON 31 DECEMBER
(In £m)

Assets	1985	1986	1987
Current assets			
Cash	9	13	13
Marketable securities	18	22	20
Debts	86	105	112
Stock	117	153	202
Income-tax refunds receivable	—	—	1
Prepaid expenses	3	5	4
Total current assets	233	298	352
Plant property and equipment	27	37	36
Other assets	6	6	5
Deferred charges	1	1	1
Total	267	342	394

Liabilities			
	1985	1986	1987
Current liabilities			
Unsecured notes and current portion of long-term debt	57	69	80
Creditors	17	22	24
Accrued expenses	11	17	16
Taxation	12	9	11
Total current liabilities	97	117	131
Long-term debt	47	95	125
Other liabilities	—	1	2
Deferred taxes	2	2	1
Deferred income	1	1	1
Debentures	5	5	5
Total liabilities	152	221	265
Minority interest	7	9	11
Shareholders' equity	108	112	118
	267	342	394

J SMITH LTD
INCOME STATEMENT

For years ending 31 December
(£m)

	1985	1986	1987
Net sales	178	215	230
Less cost of sales	125	148	161
Gross income	53	65	69
Selling, general and administrative expenses	33	40	48
Research & Development	6	7	3
Operating income	14	19	18
Interest income	3	2	4
Other income	1	1	2
Other expenses	(2)	(1)	(1)
Earnings before interest and tax	16	21	23
Interest expense	4	3	4
Pretax income	12	18	19
Tax	5	6	6
Net income (NI) before extraordinary items	7	12	13
Extraordinary gain/(loss)	3	—	2
NI after extraordinary item	10	12	15
Equity in NI of unconsolidated subsidiary	1	1	2
	11	13	17
Minority interest in consolidated subsidiary	4	5	7
Net income	7	8	10

J SMITH LTD
SOURCES AND USES OF FUNDS

(£m)

Sources	1985	1986	1987
Operating net income	7	8	10
Non-cash items:			
Depreciation	4	5	5
Non-current deferred	1	—	—
Tax			
Others	3	—	2
Funds from operations	15	13	17
Change in net working	(29)	(47)	(53)
Investment			
Operating cash flow	(44)	(34)	(36)
Extraordinary items	3	1	2
Sale of assets	—	1	4
Other	—	1	—
Total sources	11	32	30
Uses			
Additions to plant and equipment	10	15	8
Additions to non-current investment	—	—	—
Dividends	3	—	2
Other	—	2	2
Total uses	13	27	12
Excess (deficit)	(24)	(49)	(42)
Financed By			
Short-term debt	2	10	12
Long-term debt			
Repayments	(12)	(12)	(13)
Proceeds	28	49	41
Equity	18	2	—
Cash	(4)	4	—
Marketable securities	(8)	(4)	2
	24	49	42

4. Liquidity

One of the first things a person needs to know about a company is whether it can pay its currently maturing financial obligations as well as having enough cash to meet its operational requirements. If a company cannot, it may be forced to sell its more important assets at a loss and, in extreme cases, be forced into liquidation.

Current ratio

The most common measure of liquidity is the *current ratio*. This is computed by dividing current assets by current liabilities.

Current assets consist of debtors (net of provision for bad and doubtful debts), stocks, marketable securities, prepaid expenses and other debts within one year.

Current liabilities normally include creditors, bank overdrafts, current maturities of long-term debts, accrued income taxes, accrued expenses and other obligations payable in the next twelve months.

$$\text{current ratio} = \frac{\text{current assets}}{\text{current liabilities}}$$

Global Ltd has current assets of £900,000 and current liabilities of £400,000. Its current ratio would be 2.25. This means that Global can sell its current assets at 44 per cent of its value and still pay its current creditors in full.

However, as current assets include cash and other assets that are shortly scheduled to be converted into cash, it is more than likely that a company would realise a value fairly close to its stated value.

Quick or acid test

The *quick* or *acid test* is applied to examine whether a company has adequate cash or cash equivalents to meet its current obligations without having to resort to liquidating non-cash assets such as stocks. This ratio aims to emphasise that the immediate sale of non-cash items such as stocks could be at less than its stated value, ie at a loss (distress sale). It therefore checks whether the company has adequate cash or easily realisable assets.

The *quick ratio* is calculated by dividing cash, marketable securities and debtors by current liabilities.

$$\text{quick ratio} = \frac{\text{cash and cash equivalents}}{\text{current liabilities}}$$

The current assets of Ballard Ltd at 31 December 1987, were:

	£(000)
Cash	200
Marketable securities	700
Debtors	3,100
Stocks	5,000
	9,000

Its current liabilities were £5,000 and its quick ratio is:

$$\frac{200 + 700 + 3,100}{5,000} = 0.8$$

This indicates that the company cannot, with its cash or near cash assets, pay off all of its current liabilities and would need, if necessary, to sell some of its stocks to meet its current obligations.

A low ratio is not necessarily worrying because, as current obligations mature, stocks will be converted into cash.

Net current assets

Net current assets, though not strictly a ratio, is a useful measure of liquidity.

Net current assets are calculated by deducting creditors and accrued expenses from debtors and stocks. In short, net current assets are the net working capital required by a company to meet its operational requirements and support sales. The ratio of sales to net current assets indicates the amount necessary to support or maintain a certain volume of sales. A ratio of 30 per cent would mean that, should sales increase by £100,000, the company's net current assets would need to increase by £30,000. A low ratio normally indicates that a company can afford to increase sales rapidly, whereas a high ratio can mean that a company could experience difficulties in increasing and funding an increase in sales.

The sales of Economy Fuels Ltd in 1984 was £500,000. Its net current assets are:

	1986 £(000)	1987 £(000)
Trade debtors	38	44
Stocks	62	77
	100	121
Creditors	30	40
Accrued expenses	21	5
Tax payable	18	20
	50	65
Net current assets	50	56

This ratio of net current assets to sales would be:

$$0.5 \times \frac{(50,000 + 56,000) \times 100}{500,000} = 10.6 \text{ per cent.}$$

This means that for every £1m increase in sales, the net current assets of Economy Fuels Ltd would increase by £100,000. The company would need to assure itself that funds to finance this increase would be available.

Net trade cycle

The *net trade cycle* is the time a company takes to convert goods that it has purchased to cash after paying for it. It is calculated by adding the debtors turnover in days to the stock turnover in days and deducting from it the **creditors turnover in days**, ie:

$$\text{net trade cycle} = \frac{\text{average debtors} \times 365}{\text{sales}}$$

$$+ \frac{\text{average stocks} \times 365}{\text{cost of goods sold}}$$

$$- \frac{\text{average creditors} \times 365}{\text{cost of goods sold}}$$

The relevant figures of W Gibbs Ltd are:

	1987 £(000)	1988 £(000)
Sales	100	140
Cost of goods sold	80	112
Debtors	12	22
Stocks	18	24

The net trade cycle is:

	Days

Debtor turnover:

$$0.5 \times \frac{(12,000 + 22,000) \times 365}{140,000} = 44$$

Stock turnover:

$$0.5 \times \frac{(18,000 + 24,000) \times 365}{112,000} = 68$$

$$112$$

Creditor turnover:

$$0.5 \times \frac{(8,000 + 16,000) \times 365}{112,000} = 39$$

Net trade cycle (days) 73

An improving ratio can indicate greater efficiency in the managing of debtors and stocks. It can also indicate difficulty in paying creditors. It is therefore important to consider the reasons behind the figures prior to arriving at a conclusion for a change in the cycle. The longer the trade cycle, the greater the need for financing.

Defensive interval

The *defensive ratio* is used to indicate the number of days a company could theoretically remain in business without additional sales or new loans (financing). It is calculated as:

$$\text{defensive ratio} = \frac{\text{average daily cash expenditures for operating expenses}}{\text{firm's most liquid assets}}$$

In this calculation liquid assets consist of only cash and cash equivalents. Debtors and stocks are not considered because they are not the equivalent of cash. A ratio of 0.05 would indicate that a company could continue in business without liquidating any of its assets for 20 days.

The annual operating expenses of General Services Ltd are £550,000 p.a. Its current cash and cash equivalents are:

	£(000)
Cash	45
Marketable securities	105
	150

Its daily operating expenses would be

$$\frac{550,000}{365} = £1,507.$$

Its defensive interval would be

$$\frac{150,000}{1,507} = 100 \text{ days.}$$

This means that it can continue to be in business without any trade-related activity or new funding for 100 days.

Current liability coverage

This ratio, though of limited value, is used to examine the relationship between cash inflow from operations and current liabilities. In this connection, cash inflow from operations is assumed to be net income plus non-cash expenditure such as depreciation.

$$\text{current liability coverage} = \frac{\text{cash inflow from operations}}{\text{average current liabilities}}$$

This ratio indicates whether the company can meet its currently maturing obligations from internally-generated funds.

The net income of L Rumbold Ltd for the year ended 31 December 1987 was £150,000. This was arrived at after deducting depreciation of £25,000. Its current liabilities at 31 December 1986 and 31 December 1987 were £300,000 and £450,000, respectively. The current liability coverage is therefore:

$$\frac{150,000 + 25,000}{0.5 \times (300,000 + 450,000)} = 0.46$$

This means that the cash flow from operations is only 46 per cent of current liabilities and if the liabilities are to be paid out of the cash generated from operations, it would take the company a little over two years to do so.

Summary

As a company begins to experience financial difficulties, it pays its bills more slowly. This results in the build-up of current liabilities. If current liabilities are rising faster than the build-up of current assets, it could result in the company's facing financial trouble and inability to meet its obligations. Hence, a deterioration in the current ratio should cause concern.

However, a negative current ratio need not necessarily be bad. Many concerns such as fast food restaurant chains and supermarkets, which have very high stock turnover and sell for cash, normally have high current liabilities compared with current assets. This does not mean that these concerns are illiquid. It is, therefore, impossible to generalise on the ideal ratio that a company should have. Liquidity ratios will vary from industry to industry and from company to company.

It must also be remembered that before companies actually crash they become more liquid because stocks and fixed assets are sold and become converted into cash. At the same time, current liabilities decrease as creditors are paid off. It is worth remembering that expanding companies are often cash-constrained while contracting ones are often cash-rich.

In assessing the liquidity of a company, an analyst must always examine the asset quality, ie the assets that constitute the current assets. The items to check are:

- whether the current assets are stated at its currently realisable value;
- whether 'fictitious' or deferred assets such as deferred advertising expenditure are included in current assets. As these assets do not have any encashable value, they should not be considered in the calculation of the liquidity ratios.

The liquidity ratios, like all other ratios, are susceptible to window-dressing. Companies have been known to sell stocks at depressed prices at a year end in order to show greater liquidity. It is important, therefore, to look for the trends.

A large current ratio is not necessarily good. It may indicate a surplus of stocks that the company is having problems in selling at a profit. It may also be a sign of gross inefficiency in the control of asset levels. Debtor collection efforts may be weak or the company may have too much cash on its balance-sheet that it is unable to invest due to a lack of attractive opportunities.

Liquidity should, therefore, be at optimum levels rather than at highest levels. Optimum level will vary from company to company and industry to industry.

The purpose of the liquidity ratios is to assess the company's ability to pay its currently maturing obligations. The liquidity ratios are not important when considering the repayment of longer-term liabilities or where loan repayments are from the sale of assets.

5. Debt Service Capacity

A major concern for a creditor, an investor or an analyst is whether the company being analysed can service its debts, ie generate enough profit to be able to pay the interest on its loans.

The basic assumption in the *debt service capacity ratios* is that a company is a going concern and that the debt will be repaid out of internally-generated funds and not from the sale of assets or additional borrowings. The ratios therefore indicate the relationship between cash flow (internally-generated funds) and the company's liabilities.

Debt coverage

The *debt coverage ratio* indicates the time it would take for a company to repay its short- and long-term debt from internally-generated funds or profits. It is of importance if loans are to be repaid from operating income and is of limited value if the repayment is to be from the sale of assets. In this context, internally generated funds are the net profit after tax plus non-cash expenses such as depreciation less non-cash income such as the profit from the sale of fixed assets. Debts would include bank overdrafts, notes payable (both short- and long-term) and term loans. In many instances this ratio is calculated, including long-term debentures, as debt. Internally-generated funds are divided by debt or borrowed funds.

$$\text{debt coverage ratio} = \frac{\text{internally generated funds}}{\text{average debt}}$$

A ratio of 0.108 indicates that it would take a company 9.25 years to repay its borrowed funds (debts) from its internally-generated funds.

The internally-generated funds of W Nelson Ltd for the year ended 31 December 1987, was £75,000. Its debts on 31 December 1986 and 31 December 1987 were £900,000 and £850,000, respectively. Its debt coverage is:

$$\frac{75,000}{0.5 \times (900,000 + 850,000)} = 0.086$$

This shows that it would take the company 11 years to pay its current liabilities through internally-generated funds.

This ratio is especially relevant if one is considering extending credit or a short-term loan which is to be repaid through internally-generated funds.

Liability coverage

The *liability coverage ratio* is used to determine the time a company would take to pay off all its liabilities from internally-generated funds. This assumes that liabilities will not be liquidated from additional borrowings or from the sale of assets. It is calculated by dividing internally-generated funds by average total liabilities.

$$\text{liability coverage ratio} = \frac{\text{internally-generated funds}}{\text{total average liabilities}}$$

If the ratio for a company was 0.20 it would indicate that the company could pay off all its liabilities in 5 years. On the other hand, a ratio of 0.125 would mean that it would take the company 8 years to pay off its liabilities in full.

The total liabilities of S Roberts Ltd on 31 December 1987, and 31 December 1988 were £1,250,000 and £1,400,000, respectively. Its internally-generated funds in 1984 were £95,000. Its liability coverage ratio is, therefore:

$$\frac{95,000}{0.5 \times (1,250,000 + 1,400,000} = 0.0717$$

The company would therefore take 13.95 years to pay its total liabilities.

This ratio is also often calculated by considering only the liabilities at the date of the balance-sheet on the argument that the thing to be considered is the time it would take to pay off the total liabilities at a particular time.

The liability coverage ratio is susceptible to window-dressing as liabilities on the balance-sheet date can be reduced either by paying them or by suppressing them.

Interest cover

The *interest cover ratio* is a ratio of prime importance to a creditor. It measures whether a company has adequate profits to meet the interest payments on its obligations. It is arrived at by dividing a company's earnings before interest and tax (EBIT) by its interest expense:

$$\text{interest cover ratio} = \frac{\text{earnings before interest and tax}}{\text{interest expense}}$$

A cover ratio of two times would indicate that its earnings before its interest expense are twice that of its expense and can, therefore, meet its obligations. Conversely, should the interest expense be more than its earnings, it would cause concern to a creditor as the earnings would not be able to service the debt.

Island Oil Ltd's income statement included the following:

	£(000)
Earnings before interest and tax	800
Interest expense	420
Pre-tax income	380

The interest cover is $\dfrac{800,000}{420,000} = 1.95$

The company's earnings before interest and tax are nearly double its interest expense.

This ratio is very important as it checks whether the profits of a company can meet its interest commitments. It must always be measured prior to the extension of a loan as one must be satisfied whether the loan can be serviced.

Fixed charge cover

Many companies prefer, as opposed to assuming debt, to resort to what is normally known as *off balance-sheet financing*. This means that instead of purchasing an item of machinery or a building they prefer to lease them. The lease rent paid, like interest, is charged to operating expenses.

Fixed charge cover considers whether the company makes sufficient income before interest and rental expenses to meet its interest and rental obligations and shows the relationship between earnings and cost of debt and fixed charges.

$$\text{fixed charge cover} = \frac{\text{EBIT and rental expenses}}{\text{interest and rental expense}}$$

In order to fully consider fixed charges, one should also take into account preferred dividends. As preferred dividends are an appropriation of income, the fixed charge cover can also be calculated as:

$$\frac{\text{Net income} + (1 - \text{tax rate})\ (\text{interest and rental expenses})}{(1 - \text{tax rate})\ (\text{interest and rental expenses}) + \text{preferred dividends}}$$

W W Walker Ltd's earnings before interest and tax was £850,000. Its rental and interest expense are £500,000 and £400,000, respectively. The fixed cover ratio is:

$$\frac{850{,}000 + 500{,}000}{500{,}000 + 400{,}000} = 1.5$$

This means that the company generates adequate income to pay its interest and rent expenses.

This ratio is a purer measure than the interest cover ratio as it considers the fixed obligations that a company has and examines whether earnings are sufficient.

Summary

Debt service ratios are of prime importance to lenders as they enable them to determine whether a company has the capacity/ability to service its debts and repay its liabilities. Companies whose earnings before interest and tax are equal or less than the interest expense that it has to bear are risky from the lender's point of view because the loan itself can become doubtful. Similarly, a company that is intending to pay its debts through its operating cash flow should be able to demonstrate that it can do so.

6. Asset Management or Efficiency

Asset management or *efficiency ratios* are calculated to consider how effectively a company is managing its assets. It allows an analyst to consider and examine whether the total amount of each type of asset a company has is reasonable, too high or too low in the light of current and forecast operating needs. In order to purchase assets companies may need to obtain additional external finance. Thus, if there are more assets than necessary, the interest expense would be high and profits lower than otherwise. Conversely, should there be fewer assets than necessary, the company's operations would not be as efficient as possible.

The asset management ratio assumes that sales volumes are related to assets over time. Ratios can be used to assess trends and the efficiency with which the management of a company utilises its assets. This can be compared with that of the rest of the industry and with other companies. It should be remembered that a high asset turnover is not necessarily indicative of a high return on investment. It could indicate that a company is not keeping adequate levels of assets which could affect its performance in the long run.

Asset management or efficiency ratios are very useful too in making financial statement forecasts.

Stock turnover

The *stock turnover ratio* measures the number of times stock is turned over in a year or the number of days stocks are held by a company to support sales. This ratio is calculated by either:

$$\text{stock turnover ratio} = \frac{\text{cost of goods sold}}{\text{average stock}} = \text{times stock turned over}$$

or:

> stock turnover ratio = $\dfrac{365 \times \text{average stock}}{\text{cost of goods sold}}$ = stock measured in days of sale

A ratio of 6 times or 60 days indicates that enough stock to support sales for 60 days is held by the company.

The ratios enable an analyst to examine whether the company holds excessive stocks. Excessive stocks are unproductive and represent an investment with a low or zero rate of return. Conversely, if a company has less stock than it should, it could result in a loss of customers which would offset the advantage of having low stock.

It should be noted that if stocks are stated at market value, the ratio should be calculated using sales and not the cost of sales.

The average stock held by S J Dill Ltd in 1986 and 1987 was £89,000 and £83,000, respectively. During this period, its cost of goods sold was £620,000 and £700,000 respectively. Its stock turnover ratio is, therefore:

1986 $\dfrac{89,000}{620,000} \times 365 = 52$ days

1987 $\dfrac{83,000}{700,000} \times 365 = 43$ days

The stock turnover has increased and the efficiency has improved. However, stock levels are supporting higher sales. The analyst must check that the improvement has not been as a result of dumping stock on dealers etc.

Average collection period

The *average collection period ratio* represents the length of time a company must wait after making a sale before it actually receives cash from its customers. The ratio is calculated by either:

> average collection period ratio = $\dfrac{\text{average debts}}{\text{average sales per day}}$

or:

> average collection period ratio = $\dfrac{\text{average debts} \times 365}{\text{sales}}$

This ratio is important in assessing the effectiveness of the credit administration of a company. If credit is normally given for 30 days and the ratio indicates an average collection period of 42 days, it indicates that customers are not paying in time. It also enables the management to take timely measures to control and effectively manage credit.

All increasing ratio can also indicate that the company is experiencing difficulties in collecting debts. This could be an early warning sign for large bad debts.

The average debts of L Warren Ltd in 1986 and 1987 were £45,000 and £55,000, respectively. The sales during those years were £500,000 and £540,000, respectively. The average collection period during the years were:

1986 $\dfrac{45,000}{500,000} \times 365 = 33 \text{ days}$

1987 $\dfrac{55,000}{540,000} \times 365 = 37 \text{ days}$

The increasing ratio could indicate that the company is either:

- extending longer credit terms to increase sales; or
- having difficulty in collecting its debts.

The actual reason should be investigated.

Fixed asset utilisation

The *fixed asset utilisation ratio* measures the effectiveness of a company's utilisation of its fixed assets. It measures whether a company uses its fixed assets to as high a percentage of capacity as other firms in the industry and is calculated as follows:

> fixed asset utilisation ratio = $\dfrac{\text{sales}}{\text{net fixed assets}}$

A low rate may be indicative of an expanding firm preparing for future growth. On the other hand, it may also be that a company has cut back on capital expenditure as its near-term outlook is bad.

The ratio is not truly reflective of performance because if a company had purchased capital assets recently, the ratio would be high, whereas if its fixed assets are very old, its ratio would be low. This cannot be interpreted as the company being more efficient.

Total asset utilisation

The *total asset utilisation ratio* is used to examine whether a company is generating a sufficient volume of business taking into consideration the size of its asset investment. This ratio is computed by dividing sales by the average total assets:

$$\text{total asset utilisation ratio} = \frac{\text{sales}}{\text{average total assets}}$$

The ratio measures the financial productivity of assets. If a company had recently purchased fixed assets, the ratio would tend to be low whereas if its assets were old (and highly depreciated) the ratio would be high.

The total asset utilisation ratios of Grim Bros Ltd in 1986 and 1987 were 3.8 and 4.2, respectively. This indicates that the assets required to support a level of sales have decreased. The reasons for the improvement must be investigated.

Net current assets

Net current assets are defined as those matters which are directly affected by sales, eg as debtors, stocks and trade creditors. The ratio is calculated as:

$$\text{net current assets ratio} = \frac{\text{net current assets}}{\text{sales}}$$

This ratio indicates the liquidity of non-financial companies and the operational working capital requirements of a company. It also shows how efficiently working investments are being managed and controlled.

The net current assets ratio shows a company's need for working capital and its relation to the volume of business a company handles. If the ratio was £0.30, it would indicate that for every £100 growth in sales, net current assets will increase by £30 to support the increased sales, suggesting to the management that additional financing would be necessary to support the increase in sales.

Creditor ratio

The *creditor ratio* shows the period of time the company takes to pay its trade creditors and is calculated as follows:

$$\text{creditor ratio} = \frac{\text{creditors}}{\text{cost of goods sold}} \times 365$$

This ratio could indicate whether the company is taking more time than usual to pay or if it is having difficulty in paying. It would also indicate whether the company is taking full advantage of credit facilities given to it.

The financial statements of B Doll Ltd included the following figures:

	1985	1986	1987
	£(000)	£(000)	£(000)
Cost of goods sold	400	420	480
Creditors	43	49	46

The ratio is:

$$1986 \quad 0.5 \times \frac{(43,000 + 49,000)}{420,000} \times 365 = 40 \text{ days}$$

$$1987 \quad 0.5 \times \frac{(49,000 + 46,000)}{480,000} \times 365 = 36 \text{ days}$$

This ratio has decreased. This could indicate that the company

- is not being extended the credit that it had previously received; or
- it is not availing itself of its credit.

The reasons would need to be ascertained.

Summary

Asset management ratios reflect the efficiency of management and their ability to manage the assets of the company. It indicates the effectiveness of a company's credit policies, the demand for its products and can reflect to an extent whether it is having difficulty in meeting its obligations. The asset management ratios are, therefore, very important in understanding a company.

It must be remembered that a deterioration in ratios is not necessarily bad. The creditor ratio may decrease as a company is paying earlier to obtain a cash discount. It may be extending longer credit terms in order to increase sales. Stocks may have increased as the company is expanding its facilities. Hence, asset management ratios give pointers to the areas one should examine prior to determining the efficiency of a company.

7. Gearing or coverage

Gearing is a measure as to the extent assets are covered by liabilities. Companies with a high gearing can afford less reduction in asset values at the time of liquidation.

It is also a measure of the extent to which loans and liabilities are a source of funds. Creditors look to equity or owners' funds to see the owners' stake in the company, the owners' abiding commitment and to provide them (the creditors) with a margin of safety. If the owners have provided only a small proportion of the finance of the company, then the major risks are borne by the creditors. The owners, by financing the company with outside loans, control the firm with limited investment.

Gearing indicates the level of financial risk which is being borne in addition to the business risk.

It is also a very important measure in assessing credit risk. If a company is very dependent on borrowed funds, profits will be high during years of growing profitability, but in a bad year, they will be low and could even be at a loss. This is illustrated on page 38.

It will be observed from the illustration that so long as the return or the rate of profit exceeds the cost of borrowed funds, the highly geared is more profitable. However, should the trend reverse, should sales decrease or costs increase or depression set in, the income generated by highly-geared firms are used almost entirely to service their debt and the return to shareholders becomes negligible.

In short, if a company earns more on borrowed funds than it pays in interest, the return on owners' funds are magnified. If the operating income is low, the financial gearing will reduce the equity return below the rate of return on assets. In this instance, *return on equity* is measured as:

$$\text{return on equity} = \frac{\text{income available on common shareholders}}{\text{common equity}}$$

	Company A £(000)	Company B £(000)	Company C £(000)
Share capital	20	80	100
Borrowed funds at 15% p.a.	80	20	—
	100	100	4
Good year:			
EBIT	50	50	50
Interest paid at 15%	12	3	—
	38	47	50
Tax at 50%	19	23	25
	19	23	25
Return to ordinary Shareholders (%)			
Before tax	190	58.75	50
After tax	85	29.38	25
Reasonable year:			
EBIT	30	30	30
Interest paid at 15% pa	12	3	—
	18	27	30
Tax at 50%	9	13	15
	9	13	15
Return to ordinary shareholders %			
Before tax	90	33.75	30
After tax	45	16.88	15
Bad Year:			
EBIT	12	12	12
Interest paid at 15% pa	12	3	—
	—	9	12
Tax at 50%	—	4	6
	—	4	6
Return to ordinary shareholders %			
Before tax		11.25	12
After tax		5.63	6

Hence, companies with a low amount of debt have less risk of a loss when the economy is in recession and demand is low. Similarly, they have also lower expected returns when the economy booms. Companies with a high gearing run the risk of large losses, but they also have the opportunity of earning high profits.

Liabilities to assets

The *liabilities to assets ratio*, which is a relatively pure measure of asset coverage, indicates the total funds provided by creditors to the business: the extent the firm is financed by persons/entities other than shareholders. Liabilities in this connection include both current and long-term liabilities. Assets, on the other hand, are total assets, less intangible assets such as goodwill and deferred assets.

$$\text{liabilities to assets ratio} = \frac{\text{total liabilities}}{\text{total assets}}$$

Total liabilities	150
Shareholders' equity	50
	200
Current assets	130
Fixed assets	60
Intangible assets	10
	200

The liabilities to assets ratio is:

$$\frac{150}{190} = 0.789$$

Assets could be sold at 78.9 per cent of their book value and the company can still meet its commitments.

Debt to assets

The *debt to assets ratio* measures how well debt or borrowed funds are covered by assets and the extent to which assets can depreciate in value and still meet commitments in regard to external debt or borrowed funds. Debt is defined in this instance as borrowed funds plus capital leases and subordinated debentures. Assets in this computation are total assets less intangible assets such as goodwill and deferred assets (preliminary expenses not yet written off etc).

$$\text{debts to assets ratio} = \frac{\text{total debt}}{\text{total tangible net assets}}$$

Relevant data regarding S J Dill Ltd are:

	£(000)
Borrowed funds	50
Capital leases	20
Subordinated debentures	20
Total assets	140
Goodwill	5

The debt to assets ratio would be:

$$\frac{90,000}{135,000} \times 100 = 66.67 \text{ per cent.}$$

This indicates that assets can reduce by at least 33 per cent before the company ceases to be able to meet its commitments.

The analyst must always, at the time of calculating this ratio, examine contingent liabilities such as legal suits against the company, guarantees given, etc, and should these be material and capable of crystallising, they should be included in the calculation of the ratio.

Creditors normally prefer low debt ratios since the lower the ratio, the greater the cushion against creditors' losses in the event of a liquidation or a fall in demand and low profits.

Owners, on the other hand, may seek high gearing, either:

- to magnify earnings; or
- because selling new stock means giving up some degree of control.

Debt to net worth

The *debt to net worth ratio* indicates the extent a company is financed by out-side or borrowed funds. Debt would include subordinated debt as well as senior debt and capital leases. Net worth is arrived at by deducting intangible assets from the shareholders' equity.

$$\text{debt to net worth ratio} = \frac{\text{debt}}{\text{net worth}}$$

	£(000)
Borrowed funds (debt)	40
Shareholders' equity	15
Intangible assets	2

The debt to net worth ratio is: $\dfrac{40,000}{15,000-2,000} = \dfrac{40,000}{13,000} = 3.08$

This means that borrowed funds are three times more than the share-holders' equity in the company and that for every £3 borrowed, the share-holders have only £1 interest in the company.

In a highly geared company during bad years (recession, etc), the profits may be insufficient. A highly-geared company can also face difficulty in obtaining refinance.

Liabilities to net worth

The *liabilities to net worth ratio* measures the extent a company is financed by liabilities. It is a more useful ratio that debt to net worth as it includes all the liabilities of the company. Net worth is in the interests of conservative analysis arrived at after deducting goodwill and other intangible assets.

$$\text{liabilities to net worth ratio} = \frac{\text{total liabilities}}{\text{net worth}}$$

	£(000)
Current liabilities	25
Long-term liabilities	80
Total liabilities	105
Shareholders' equity	45
	150
Tangible assets	145
Intangible assets	5
	150

The liability to net worth ratio is: $\dfrac{105}{45-5} = 2.625$

This ratio includes both interest and non-interest-bearing liabilities of a firm. This ratio is more realistic because, at the time a company is being liquidated, all senior liabilities such as trade creditors and wages due are paid along with unsecured borrowings, with no particular preferential treatment.

In the above ratio, liabilities are 72 per cent of tangible assets and 2.63 times of net worth. In short, 72 per cent of the assets of the company are financed by liabilities.

A more conservative ratio is:

$$\frac{\text{total liabilities} + \text{capitalised operating leases}}{\text{tangible net worth}}$$

This assumes that operating leases are alternative to debt financing and argues, therefore, that this should be included in assessing a company's dependence on external funds in financing its assets.

Incremental gearing

This ratio measures the additional gearing required to finance the growth of the company. This is calculated as:

$$\text{incremental gearing} = \frac{\text{net increase in debt}}{\text{increase in net income after tax and before dividend}}$$

	1987 £(000)	1988 £(000)
Net income after tax but before dividend	180	200
Debt	1,000	1,300

The incremental gearing is:

$$\frac{1,300-1,000}{200-180} = £15$$

This means that to finance every £1 growth in net inome, the debt would increase by £15.

Other gearing ratios

There are other ratios of gearing such as:

$$\text{long-term debt ratio} = \frac{\text{long-term liabilities}}{\text{long-term liabilities} + \text{shareholders' equity}}$$

$$\text{liability to equity ratio} = \frac{\text{total liabilities}}{\text{total liabilities} + \text{shareholders' equity}}$$

Based on the figures shown on p. 42, these ratios are shown as follows:

Long-term debt ratio $= \dfrac{80}{80 \times 45} = 0.64$

Liability to equity ratio $= \dfrac{105}{105 + 45} = 0.70$

These show the relationship that long-term liabilities and total liabilities have to shareholders' funds and the extent to which liabilities finance the company.

Summary

The gearing ratios indicate whether a company has overborrowed, whether it has the capacity to obtain additional funds and the effects on the profits of gearing. Gearing must be examined and studied in detail when analysing a company.

The importance of gearing is appreciated when it is realised that if, during a period of growth, a company borrows extensively, it can collapse should a recession occur and sales and profits fall. Furthermore, to a lender, a higher geared company has less capacity to obtain refinance than one that is not geared and therefore becomes riskier.

8. Earnings

The *earnings ratio*, with its variations, indicates the earnings available per ordinary share. It is an indicator which enables investors and shareholders to judge the earnings per share of a company and is often considered an indicator of profitability.

Earnings per share

The *earnings per share* show an investor the earnings attributable to an ordinary share in a year.

$$\text{earnings per share} = \frac{\text{income attributable to ordinary shareholders}}{\text{weighted average of ordinary share}}$$

In 1987, the income attributable to ordinary shareholders in D Sutton Ltd was £50,000. On 1 January 1987 the company had a balance of 25,000 ordinary shares of £1 each. On 31 March 1987 the company issued a further 12,000 shares. The earnings per share in 1987 were:

$$\frac{50,000}{25,000} = \text{£2 per share.}$$

$$\frac{50,000}{25,000 + \dfrac{(9 \text{ months} \times 12,000)}{(12 \text{ months})}} = \text{£1.47}$$

This ratio has been further varied to show the fully-diluted earnings per share. This is the earnings per share that would occur if all share options, warrants and convertible securities outstanding at the end of the accounting period were exchanged for ordinary shares.

The earnings per share ratio has been criticised as a measure of profitability on the argument that it does not consider the amount of assets, finance or capital required to generate a particular amount of income.

Dividend payout

The *dividend payout ratio* shows the amount of dividend paid out of earnings. It gives an indication of the amount of profit put back into the company and is an important ratio when assessing the long-term prospects of a company.

$$\text{dividend payout ratio} = \frac{\text{dividend}}{\text{net income}}$$

In 1987, the net income of Property Assets Ltd was £580,000 and the dividend paid by the company was £260,000.

The dividend payout ratio is:

$$\frac{260,000}{580,000} = 0.448$$

This shows that the company is paying out nearly 45 per cent of its income as divdend. This is a fairly high payout and can be worrying as in difficult years the company could have problems of liquidity. Furthermore, there may not be adequate funds for expansion when the need arises.

Summary

The earnings ratios are not indicators of the profitability of a company, but they give an analyst an idea of the policies of a company such as the amount of income ploughed back into the company and the earnings per share earned. It gives him an indication as to the directions the company intends to go—whether it believes in expansion from internally-generated funds or from borrowed funds. This, in turn, will determine the relative safety of funds lent.

9.   Market Value

The market value ratios are important both to investors and to the company. It gives an indication to investors of the reputation of a company in financial circles and the length of time it will take for their investment to be recouped. It gives the company's management an idea of what investors and financial experts think of the company's past performance and future prospects. If a firm's liquidity, asset management, debt management and profitability ratios are all good, then its market value ratios and stock price will be high.

Price/earnings

The *price/earnings ratio* shows how long it would take to recover the cost of an investment. It is calculated as follows:

$$price/earnings\ ratio = \frac{market\ price\ per\ share}{dividend\ per\ share}$$

The dividend paid for the year ended 31 December 1987, was £1 and the market value was £32. The price/earnings ratio is:

$$\frac{32}{1} = 32$$

This means that it would take an investor 32 years to get back his investment.

Usually, the price/earnings ratio of long, well-established and financially-sound companies are high, whereas in weaker ones, as the returns commensurate with the risks are higher, the price/earnings ratio is low.

Market to book

The *market to book ratio* indicates the value investors place on the company. It can also suggest in certain situations that the assets of a company are understated. The market to book ratio is calculated as follows:

$$\text{market to book ratio} = \frac{\text{market price per share}}{\text{book value per share}}$$

In 1987, the market price per share of Biggs Bros was £23.40. The book value of its share was £21.20.

Its market/book ratio was:

$$\frac{23.40}{21.20} = 1.10$$

The company's value in the market place is 10 per cent higher than its actual book value. This may be because:

- its assets are understated;
- its prospects are good and investors believe that its earnings and value would grow.

Summary

Market value ratios can be misleading because in a boom period the ratios may be high, while in a depression they may be low. Their importance to investors is thus of limited value as they do not reveal the profitability or efficiency of a company but merely indicates the company's reputation in the market place.

It should also be stressed that book values are based on historical cost accounting convention and balance sheets are not intended to be statements of current value. Therefore, any conclusions drawn from comparisons of book values to market values should be treated with great caution.

PART II
Using ratios to evaluate banks and financial institutions

10. Basis of Analysis

The income statements and balance sheets of banks and financial institutions are very different from those of commercial companies. The assets and liabilities of a bank are invariably monetary by nature. Commercial and industrial companies will have, however, fixed and other assets which, while of value in monetary terms, can also be in the form of buildings, stock, work in progress, etc. The financial statements of Minton Bank are attached to give an indication of their layout. It will be noticed that the biggest asset and liability are loans and deposits, respectively.

Because of the nature of the business of banking and the regard in which banks and financial institutions are held, their analysis appears awesome. Their problems are often considered to be in a different league from those which plague industrial and commercial concerns. The phrase often used to describe a thriving and prosperous company is 'as solid as a bank'. This, in reality, is not always the truth. Banks have crashed and banks have fallen on hard times so it is important for an investor thinking of investing in a bank, or a banker considering lending to another bank or for a supplier or a depositor to analyse the bank concerned to ascertain the safety of his money.

Bank ratio analysis aims at determining the risks that could arise for depositors, creditors or shareholders when dealing with a bank. The risks are mainly focused on the liabilities and the operating results of a bank. This is because a bank's ability to attract and retain deposits and other sources of funds is the main risk in banking. The ratio analysis really deals with the possibility of deposits and borrowings being recalled. If the return is low, there is a great risk of a flight of deposits and other sources of funds.

Ratios, therefore, normally focus on changes in operations and circumstances that change risk and increase or decrease safety of funds deposited/lent. The factors that influence the risk of a bank are its operating results, its quality of assets, the stability of liabilities, the composition of assets and liabilities and shareholders' funds. Because of this, the ratios in this section are grouped under the following classifications:

- profitability;
- liquidity;
- asset quality;
- capital adequacy.

MINTON BANK

INCOME STATEMENT FOR THE YEARS
ENDED 31 DECEMBER (£m)

Income	1988	1987
Interest income	2,000	1,965
Interest expense	1,621	1,583
Net interest income	379	382
Commission and fees	230	189
Income from investments	60	80
Foreign exchange income	100	95
Other income	8	6
Net financial revenue	777	752
Expenditure		
Salaries	182	169
Other operating expenses	201	198
Total operating expenses	383	367
Income before provisions and taxes	394	385
Provisions	28	24
Income tax	100	92
Income after tax	266	269
Dividends	80	75
	186	194

MINTON BANK

BALANCE SHEET AS ON 31 DECEMBER (£m)

ASSETS	1988	1987
Cash at Central Bank and in hand	1,072	982
Due from banks (short term)	235	112
Investments	1,970	1,971
Bills discounted	889	920
Loans and advances	3,903	3,022
Acceptances (Contra)	1,012	1,132
Total banking assets	9,081	8,139
Fixed assets	421	434
Other assets	376	362
Total assets	9,878	8,935
LIABILITIES		
Demand deposits	1,679	1,432
Time and savings deposits	4,544	4,421
Total deposits	6,223	5,853
Due to banks	1,784	1,279
Acceptances (Contra)	1,012	1,132
Other liabilities	266	264
Total liabilities	9,285	8,528
Stockholders' capital	593	407
Total liabilities and capital	9,878	8,935

11. Profitability

Profits are the lifeblood of commercial enterprises. It is profits that attract and retain capital. They are necessary for growth, development and the very survival of all institutions. They are also a measure of the competence and ability of management.

A growth in income and assets and the returns a bank earns instils confidence in a bank and attracts new funds to it, be it deposits, borrowed funds or stockholders' equity. This helps to support its growth in assets.

It is imperative, therefore, that the profitability of a bank be examined. In calculating profitability ratios, it is important that they be calculated on average assets and liabilities. This is because profits are earned over a period of time. If the ratios are calculated on balances that are not average, the figures will be distorted and misleading.

Return on assets

The *return on assets* is a major measure of profitability and enables an analyst to determine whether:

- the return earned is comparative to that earned by other similar banks;
- the assets of the bank are efficiently utilised.

This ratio is calculated in the following manner:

$$\text{return on assets} = \frac{\text{net income before securities gains and losses}}{\text{average total assets}}$$

The 1987 financial statement of Minton Bank included the following figures:

	1987 £(000)	1988 £(000)
Net income before security gains and losses	450	500
Average total assets	35,000	40,000

The return on assets is:

1987 $\dfrac{450,000}{35,000,000} \times 100 = 1.29$ per cent.

1988 $\dfrac{500,000}{40,000,000} \times 100 = 1.25$ per cent.

The return on assets has fallen marginally in 1988. This does not in itself mean that 1988 was a bad year. The reasons may include:

- the loan portfolio may be more conservative;
- non-recurring losses may have been written off.

The analyst must determine the reasons for a change in the return and compare it with the return earned by other banks.

Return on equity

The *return on equity* shows the return earned on stockholders' investment in a bank. It enables an analyst to determine whether the return made is, in a given situation, the best available.

$$\text{return on equity} = \frac{\text{net income before securities gains and losses}}{\text{average stockholders' equity}}$$

An extract of the financial statements of Safety Bank reads:

	1987 £(000)	1988 £(000)
Net income	183	192
Securities gains (losses)	81	28
	264	164
Average stockholders' equity	1,000	1,100

The return on equity is:

1987 $\dfrac{183,000}{1,000,000} \times 100 = 18.3$ per cent.

1988 $\dfrac{192,000}{1,100,000} \times 100 = 17.5$ per cent.

In 1988, although the income earned was greater in value terms, the return was lower due to the change in average stockholders' equity.

In 1988, the stockholders received a return on their investment of 17.5 per cent. If other banks or companies yield a higher return, then it would indicate that the return earned by Safety Bank is low, unless there is some other factor that has caused a low return. Similarly, if the return is very high in comparison with other similar banks, then the analyst must examine the reason and be satisfied that the return stated is correct.

Net interest margin

The *net interest margin ratio* measures the spread (interest income, less interest expense) earned on interest-bearing assets. It is arrived at by dividing interest income less interest-bearing or earning assets as follows:

$$\text{net interest margin ratio} = \frac{\text{interest income less interest expense}}{\text{average gross interest-bearing assets}}$$

(It is important to use average daily assets in the computation of this ratio as average earning assets change quite materially from day to day.)

The financial statements of Long Bank included the following:

	1987 £(000)	1988 £(000)
Interest income	83	989
Interest expense	799	949
	33	40
Average interest-bearing assets	8,837	9,285

The net interest margin was:

1987 $\dfrac{33,000}{8,837,000} \times 100 = 0.37$ per cent.

1988 $\dfrac{40,000}{9,285,000} \times 100 = 0.43$ per cent.

The margin improved slightly in 1988. It should be remembered that a low margin is not bad in itself. It may indicate investment in relatively low-risk assets. Some banks that deal with large institutions or corporations lend at very low spreads because the client is financially strong.

On the other hand a high return may suggest that a bank has lent to high-risk clients or that the bank is mainly in retail banking with a large deposit base.

Hence, after calculating the margin, it is important to examine the reasons for its size to evaluate the performance of the bank properly.

This ratio also gives a good idea of the capabilities of a management in earning a good spread.

Gross interest margin

The *gross interest margin* is used to examine the spread earned on income. This is a very useful measure in determining the profitability of transactions and is calculated as follows:

$$\text{gross interest margin} = \frac{\text{interest income}-\text{interest expense}}{\text{interest income}}$$

Northern Bank's financial statements included the following figures:

	1987 £(000)	1988 £(000)
Interest income	828	987
Interest expense	801	950
Net interest income	27	37

The margin is:

1987 $\dfrac{27,000}{828,000} \times 100 = 3.3$ per cent.

1988 $\dfrac{37,000}{987,000} \times 100 = 3.7$ per cent.

There has been a marginal improvement in 1988. However, the components that caused this to occur should be examined in detail to establish whether there has, in reality, been an improvement.

Gross earning asset yield

Interest rates fluctuate widely between assets, customers and so on and it is therefore not possible to state the normal return on earning assets. However, this ratio would help an analyst to determine, by comparing with other similar banks, whether a bank is charging (earning) comparable or reasonable interest rates.

This ratio is computed as:

$$\text{gross earning asset yield} = \frac{\text{interest income}}{\text{average gross earning assets}}$$

In 1988, the interest income earned by Eurocoop Bank was £788,000, whereas its average gross-earning assets were £4,690,000. Its gross-earning asset yield was, therefore:

$\dfrac{788,000}{4,690,000} \times 100 = 16.8$ per cent.

The above return should be examined against the return earned by other similar banks to establish whether the return is high or low. The assets should also be examined to check whether they are high-risk or low-risk assets.

Loan yield

The *loan yield ratio* shows the yield the bank earns on its loan portfolio and as loans are a bank's most important asset, this is a very important ratio.

This ratio is computed as:

$$\text{loan yield} = \frac{\text{loan interest income} + \text{fees} + \text{lease income}}{\text{average loans} + \text{leases}}$$

Connaught Bank's average loans plus lease in 1988 was £8,589,000. The interest and fees it earned on these loans and its lease income was £1,417,000. Its loan yield, therefore, was:

$$\frac{1,417,000 \times 100}{8,589,000} = 16.50 \text{ per cent.}$$

This yield should be compared with that of other similar banks. A very high yield could indicate that the bank is lending to high-risk customers or on high-risk ventures. A low yield, on the other hand, may be indicative of the bank's being very conservative. A sharp decline in the yield from one year to the next may be due to certain loans being written off.

Breakeven yield

The *breakeven yield* is the return the bank must get in order to meet its interest expense cost. In order that the bank may earn adequate income to meet its fixed and variable administration and other cost and earn a profit, the return earned should be in excess of the breakeven yield. The breakeven yield is arrived at by expressing interest expense as a percentage of average gross earning assets:

$$\text{breakeven yield} = \frac{\text{interest expense}}{\text{average gross earning assets}}$$

In 1988, the interest expense incurred by Hamilton Bank was £8,976,000. Its average earning during that year was £72,800,000. Its breakeven yield in 1988 was hence:

$$\frac{8{,}976{,}000 \times 100}{72{,}800{,}000} = 12.3 \text{ per cent.}$$

If it is to make a profit and meet its various expenses, the bank has to earn a yield in excess of 12.3 per cent.

As the cost of funds increase the breakeven yield will rise and this will decrease the profitability of the bank. The bank, in this instance, would need to either decide to absorb the increase or it would pass it on to the customer.

Interest rate sensitivity

All banks and financial institutions are sensitive to changes in interest rates and it is important while analysing such enterprises to examine and determine the extent of their sensitivity to changes in interest rates.

The *interest rate sensitivity ratio* is measured by relating the change in interest rates earned on earning assets to the change in interest rate suffered on interest-bearing liabilities:

$$\text{interest rate sensitivity ratio} = \frac{\text{change in interest rate on average earnings assets}}{\text{change in interest rate (cost) on average interest-bearing liabilities}}$$

A ratio of 1 indicates the bank is in balance, a ratio less than 1 shows that the bank would benefit from an interest rate decline. On the other hand, a ratio greater than 1 indicates that the bank would benefit from an increased interest rate.

In 1988, the interest rate increased by 2 per cent. The increase in cost of interest expense was 1.8 per cent. The interest rate sensitivity would be:

$$\frac{2.0 \times 100}{1.8} = 111 \text{ per cent.}$$

It will be to the bank's advantage should the rate of interest change.

Overhead

The *overhead ratio* indicates the overheads in proportion to net financial revenue. Net financial revenue is made up of net interest income, commission, fees and other income, excluding income from security gains and losses. Overheads include all recurring costs, but exclude interest expenses and provisions for loan losses.

$$\text{overheads ratio} = \frac{\text{overheads}}{\text{net financial ratio}}$$

Overheads usually range between 55 per cent and 75 per cent of net financial revenue. When evaluating banks and other financial institutions, it is important to examine this ratio in conjunction with the net interest margin. Usually, a bank with a low net interest margin has a low overhead ratio. A possible reason for high overheads may be that there are high costs in the services that generate commission, fees and other income. Conversely, overheads may be high due to high staffing or other fixed costs.
may be high due to high staffing or other fixed costs.

This ratio shows how effective a bank is in its management of expenses in running its organisation.

An extract of the financial statements of Brendon Bank was as follows:

Income	£(000)
Interest income	1,095
Interest expense	1,056
Net interest income	39
Commission and fees	52
Other income	8
Net financial revenue	99

Expenditure	£(000)
Salary and benefits	27
Administration costs	24
Other expenses	6
Total operating expenses	57
Net income	42

The overhead ratio is:

$$\frac{57}{99} = 57.6 \text{ per cent.}$$

Loan loss provision

Loan losses are a major expense for banks and the provision or lack of it for loan losses help an analyst determine the quality of the portfolio and the profitability of the bank.

Most banks provide for loan losses as a percentage of its loan portfolio and when an amount is written off, that amount is debited to the provision for loan losses account in the balance sheet. Recoveries on losses written off earlier are also credited to this account.

The analyst should examine this provision to determine whether it is adequate. The *loan loss provision ratio* to examine this can be computed by dividing the net losses written off by the provision for loan losses:

$$\text{loan loss provision ratio} = \frac{\text{loans written off} - \text{recoveries (net charged off)}}{\text{provision for loan losses}}$$

In 1988, the loans written off by Beauchamp Bank was £819,000. It recovered in that year £97,000 from loans that were previously written off. Its provision for loan losses was £1,352,000.

The loan loss provision ratio for the bank is:

$$\frac{819,000 - 97,000}{1,352,000} = 53.4 \text{ per cent.}$$

The provision for loan losses appears to be adequate to cover possible losses.

As most banks maintain their reserves for loan losses as a percentage of their loan portfolio, the provision made should really be in accordance with actual amounts written off and should not vary drastically.

If the net amounts charged off are usually more than the provision for loan losses, the likelihood exists of the income of the bank being overstated as the bank is probably not charging an adequate amount against income.

Dividend payout

The *dividend payout ratio* states as a percentage the amount of income paid out to stockholders as dividend. This ratio is useful in assessing the return earned on investments made and allows a stockholder to compare this with the dividends earned on other investments:

$$\text{dividend payout ratio} = \frac{\text{dividend}}{\text{income after tax}}$$

Meteor Bank paid a dividend of 10 per cent in 1988 on its equity share capital of £100,000m. Its net income after tax that year was £50,000m. The bank's dividend payout ratio is, therefore:

$$\frac{0.1 \times 100,000}{50,000} = 20 \text{ per cent.}$$

Meteor has distributed 20 per cent of its net income as dividend, retaining 80 per cent to strengthen its capital base.

It is difficult to state whether this ratio is good or bad. A bank may have a low payout because it is increasing its capital base. Similarly, a high payment may not be good as income may not be being ploughed back into the bank to support asset growth. This ratio is, therefore, strictly for the short-term investor who is looking for a good quick return on money invested.

12. Liquidity

Liquidity is a very important requirement for a bank because it addresses the speed at which the assets can be converted into cash.

This is one of the major concerns a depositor has when he places his savings in a bank: will he get his savings back when he wants them? It is a fear about the liquidity of a bank and its inability to repay that can lead at times to a run on a bank.

Central banks have recognised the importance of liquidity and require commercial banks to maintain a portion of their assets in easily liquid assets (usually in cash and in government securities). They further guarantee that, should a run occur, they would inject fresh cash.

In short, liquidity is important for:

- depositor and creditor confidence;
- adhering to rules of the central bank;
- meeting operating needs;
- countering contingencies such as a run.

The liquidity maintained by banks varies depending on the country in which it is operating, the regulations of the central bank, the economic environment, the kind of loans that have been given and the nature of deposits that have been received.

It should be remembered that when a bank keeps itself very liquid, its assets are usually invested in short-term, lower-interest-bearing loans/ securities or in cash. If banks are concerned about higher returns or yields, its liquidity and its vulnerability are lower. This could be dangerous in a period of depression.

However, low liquidity in itself is not dangeorus. A bank's reputation and financial condition may be such that it can relatively easily procure funds from financial institutions should a liquidity squeeze arise.

An area of potential danger is the contingent liabilities that a bank has, such as rediscounts, standby letters of credit, guarantees and litigation. In the analysis of liquidity, an analyst would be wise to consider these.

Another aspect an analyst should consider is that should the need to liquidate assets arise, the amount would be procured in their conversion to cash.

The analyst must also consider the matching of maturities, ie whether assets and liabilities mature at the same time.

Liquidity

The *liquidity ratio* aims to determine the cash or readily convertible assets available to meet demand liabilities. This is similar to the asset test done on companies. The ratio is derived by dividing cash and investments by total liabilities less stockholders' equity and long-term debt. The purpose is to check whether there will be enough liquid assets to meet the need should there be a run on deposits.

$$\text{liquidity ratio} = \frac{\text{liquid assets}}{\text{total liabilities less long-term debt and equity}}$$

An extract of the balance sheet of Ingot Bank is as follows:

	£(000)
Assets	
Cash	100
Investments	1,600
Liabilities	
Deposits	5,200
Other liabilities	200
Total liabilities	5,400

The liquidity ratio of the bank is:

$$\frac{1,100,000 + 1,600,000}{5,200,000 + 200,000} = 50 \text{ per cent.}$$

Should there be a run on the bank's deposits, the bank has only enough liquid assets to meet 50 per cent of its liabilities immediately.

Loans to deposits

The *loans to deposits ratio* is the basic measure of liquidity as it indicates the extent deposits support loans. It will reveal how difficult or easy it would be to repay deposits should the need arise.

The ratio is arrived at by dividing loans by deposits:

$$\text{loans to deposits ratio} = \frac{\text{loans}}{\text{deposits}}$$

On 31 December 1988, the balance sheet of Minton Bank Ltd showed the following figures:

Deposits	£(000)
Time Deposits	1,000
Current Account	5,500
Savings Accounts	200
	6,700

Loans	
Short-term loans	2,800
Long-term loans	3,300
	6,100

The loans/deposits ratio is:

$$\frac{6,100,000}{6,700,000} = 0.91$$

This reveals that although deposits adequately cover loans, should a run on the bank occur, the bank would need to be forced either to sell its long-term loans at a discount or to borrow funds to meet its commitments. This dependency is further illustrated by a subsidiary ratio:

$$\text{ratio} = \frac{\text{short-term loans}}{\text{short-term deposits}}$$

This ratio in the above example would be:

$$\frac{2,800,000}{5,500,000 \ + \ 200,000} \ = \ 0.49$$

The bank has short-term deposits and it has lent long term. As periods of maturity do not match, the bank could have problems should there be a withdrawal in excess of 51 per cent of its short-term deposits.

Funding ratio

In recent years, banks are increasingly becoming more dependent on borrowings. The *funding ratio*:

- indicates the extent a bank is dependent on financing loans and other assets with borrowings;
- measures the extent to which risk assets are funded by short-term borrowings and purchased liabilities.

It is assumed that borrowings are invested in both low and high-risk assets. Should borrowings exceed low-risk assets, the assumption is that the excess funds risk assets. Should low-risk assets exceed borrowings, it is assumed that risk assets are funded by some other source, such as demand and savings deposits.

The more dependent a bank is on borrowings to support risk assets, the more it is exposed if borrowings are not available.

This ratio is calculated as:

$$\text{funding ratio} = \frac{\text{borrowings} - \text{low-risk assets}}{\text{total assets} - \text{low-risk assets}}$$

In this connection, borrowings is money borowed from financial institutions, including banks and call deposits. Low-risk assets, on the other hand, are assets such as cash, government securities and so on on which the risk is minimal if not non-existent.

It should be remembered when assessing this ratio that the following should be considered:

- liability funding for the bank;
- access to funds, the experience and the competence of the bank in managing its funds and the sources of funds.

An extract of the balance sheet of First City Bank on 31 March 1988, was as follows:

Assets	£(000)
Cash	200
Marketable securities	6,000
Balances at other banks	500
Other quick assets	300
Interest fixed assets	3,000
Total assets	10,000

Liabilities	
Call deposits	2,500
Other borrowed funds	6,000

The funding ratio would be:

$$\frac{8,500 - 7,000}{10,000 - 7,000} = \frac{1,500}{3,000}$$

50 per cent of the financing of risk assets is done by purchased (borrowed) funds.

If the ratio is negative, it would mean that risk assets are being financed or funded by some other source such as deposits.

This ratio can help identify a core level of deposits and determine its growth over a period of time.

This ratio is very important as it identifies the source of funding and would show clearly the vulnerability of a bank if funding is necessary.

Time deposits of and exceeding £100,000 to total deposits

The purpose of this ratio is to determine how dependent a bank is on larger-denomination time deposits. This ratio becomes important in times of financial difficulties.

At such times, a bank dependent on large time deposits can find itself with problems should these depositors take out their money. Dependence on large deposits can also create funding problems should a transfer occur. The ratio is calculated as follows:

$$\text{ratio} = \frac{\text{large time deposits}}{\text{total deposits}}$$

The total deposits of Chambers Bank were £58,080,000 of which time deposits of £100m and more was £18,090,000. Chambers' large deposits as a percentage of total deposits was 31.1 per cent.

$$\frac{18,090,000}{58,080,000} \times 100 = 31.1 \text{ per cent.}$$

This shows a very high dependency on large deposits and the bank could be in difficulty when these deposits mature and are transferred or encashed.

13. Asset Quality

The major cause of a bank failing or a crisis in a bank is poor asset quality. It is the single most important reason for the collapse of banks, ie bad loans. Foreign exchange, deposits, maturity mismatches and open positions may cause worry and sleepless nights, but they do not normally lead to the closure of a bank. That is done by poor asset quality.

Poor asset quality, as a result of which bad loans occur, usually results from credit standards especially at the time of a very fast growth in the loan portfolio. In addition, when fraud is involved, it results from loans to owners or insiders far in excess of their entitlement or ability to repay, and from misrepresentation, bad investments, and understated liabilities.

The initial studies that can be done are by:

- examining the number of loans given to directors or others connected with the bank or to companies or businesses in which the directors or the management have an interest;
- breaking down loans to industries or to geographical areas. In times of recession, a concentration of loans to an industry undergoing a difficult period would be potentially very dangerous.

In short, asset quality essentially relates to the possibility of fluctuations in value and the effect it can have on the bank. The quality can also be assured through the record of a bank's losses: the greater the losses, the poorer the quality of the assets.

Loan loss

Poor asset quality is reflected in the loans written off or *loans loss ratio*. This ratio shows the loan loss experience of the bank in an attempt to give an analyst an idea of the quality of the assets of the bank.

If this ratio is low, it suggests that a bank has a reasonably sound portfolio and is able to recover its losses.

The ratio is calculated by dividing the net amount of loans written off by the average of the loans as follows:

$$\text{loans loss ratio} = \frac{\text{net write offs}}{\text{average total loans}}$$

The average loans of Mark bank in 1988 were £890,000. During that year, £7,500 of loans were written off. However, £1,500 was recovered from loans written off in previous years.

The loss ratio is:

$$\frac{7,500 - 1,500}{890,000} = 0.67 \text{ per cent.}$$

On average, most banks have a ratio of 0.35 to 0.45 per cent. The loss ratio of Mark Bank is very high and reflects badly on asset quality.

Non-performing loans to total loans

The *non-performing loans to total loans ratio* helps determine the quantum of non-performing loans in the total loans portfolio. (A non-performing loan is an interest-free loan.) It also gives an idea of the quality of the loan portfolio and an indication of possible loan losses in the future. The calculation is:

$$\text{non-performing loans to total loan ratio} = \frac{\text{non-performing loans}}{\text{total loans}}$$

The ratio is normally below 3 per cent. It is important, however, to examine similar banks prior to arriving at a conclusion.

The total loans of Provident Bank were £798,000. Of this, non-performing loans accounted for £32,000. The non-performing loans to total loans ratio was:

$$\frac{32,000}{798,000} = 4 \text{ per cent.}$$

This ratio is high and the analyst should examine the reasons for such a large number of non-performing loans.

Recoveries

The *recoveries ratio* is used to determine how conservative or prudent a bank is in its policy of loan write offs. This examines whether the bank has an adequate policy in regard to write offs.

$$\text{recoveries ratio} = \frac{\text{recoveries}}{\text{gross write offs}}$$

A bank that has only a 12 per cent recovery rate may only be writing off loans that are really bad. This implies that there may still be loans in the portfolio that are bad but have not been written off and should lead an analyst to wonder about the adequacy of loan loss provision and the quality of the assets.

The recoveries made by Median Bank were £50,000. Its gross write offs were £290,000. The bank's recovery ratio is:

$$\frac{50,000}{290,000} = 17 \text{ per cent.}$$

The recovery rate is not high. The analyst may want to probe deeper into the quality of the loan portfolio.

Adequacy of loan loss reserve

This ratio is examined to check whether the bank, in comparison with other similar banks, is making adequate provision for loan losses.

$$\text{loan loss reserve ratio} = \frac{\text{reserve for loan losses}}{\text{total loans}}$$

If reserve deteriorates as a result of large write offs, perhaps in excess of the provision for loan losses made in the year, then the quality of the assets will be suspect.

In 1988, the reserve for loan losses of Premium Bank was £8,000, whereas the total loans were £205,000. The adequacy ratio is:

$$\frac{8,000}{205,000} = 3.9 \text{ per cent.}$$

It is not possible to state whether this is adequate, since it depends on the quality of the assets, industry concentration of loans and the write off history of the bank.

Earnings coverage

The *earnings coverage ratio* is very important. It measures the level of earnings and the charge to income against the actual net charge offs and provides a measurement of the bank's earning cover to actual loan losses. It is prudent, therefore, when the earnings coverage is equal to or below three times, to examine and determine the reason. The ratio is calculated as follows:

$$\text{earnings coverage ratio} = \frac{\text{net operating income} + \text{provision for loan losses}}{\text{net write offs}}$$

The net operating income of Tower Bank in 1988 was £809,500. In that year, it had made a provision for loan losses of £102,000 and its net write off was £250,000. The bank's earnings coverage is:

$$\frac{809,500 - 102,000}{250,000} = 3.6 \text{ times.}$$

Its earnings are adequate to cover amounts written off.

14. Capital Adequacy

Capital adequacy ratios help the analyst to determine whether the capital of the bank is adequate.

The major thing to remember is that the capital should be adequate to absorb business risks and sustain temporary losses. This is what the capital adequacy ratios attempt to do.

Capital formation

The *capital formation ratio* is the basic measure of capital adequacy. It allows the analyst to check whether the shareholders are increasing their stake in the bank.

This ratio is arrived at by dividing retained income (net income after taxes and dividends) by the shareholders' equity at the beginning of the year:

$$\text{capital formation ratio} = \frac{\text{income after taxes} - \text{dividends}}{\text{shareholders' equity}}$$

On 1 January 1988 the shareholders' equity of Western Bank was £840m. In 1988 it earned income after taxes of £2,100,000 and distributed a dividend of £1m. The balance was retained by the bank.

The bank's capital formation rate is:

$$\frac{2,100,000 - 1,000,000}{8,400,000} = 13.1 \text{ per cent.}$$

The analyst should compare the rate of growth of the loan portfolio with the capital formation rate, because the loans are the assets of the bank that have an element of risk and the capital must support them.

The capital formation ratio can be improved either by increasing profitability or by controlling the bank's dividend policy or by controlling the growth of assets.

Capital to asset growth

The *capital to asset growth ratio* is similar to the capital formation ratio in that it examines capital formation, but it goes further. It compares it to the increase in risk assets to examine whether the increase in risk assets is cushioned by an equal increase in capital formation.

$$\text{capital asset to growth ratio} = \frac{\text{percentage increase in capital formation}}{\text{percentage increase in risk assets}}$$

In 1988, Market Bank earned an income after tax of £800,000. It distributed to its stockholders £500,000 as dividend. The stockholders' equity at the beginning of the year was £3m. During the year, its loan portfolio grew from £40m to £50m.

The capital asset growth ratio is:

$$\frac{800,000 - 500,000}{3,000,000} \times 100 = 10 \text{ per cent.}$$

Risk assets were:

$$\frac{5,000,000 - 4,000,000}{4,000,000} \times 100 = 25 \text{ per cent.}$$

Capital grew by only 10 per cent, whereas risk assets grew by 25 per cent. This makes the bank more vulnerable to losses. In ideal circumstances, the growth in risk assets and capital would have been the same.

If internally-generated capital, ie profits, cannot keep pace with the growth in risk assets, then, if the bank is to grow properly, it must consider other sources of capital such as the issue of new stock in order to avoid a deterioration in capital structure.

Gross capital to average assets plus reserves

The *gross capital to average assets ratio* is calculated to determine the extent of permanent or semi-permanent capital in the bank, as this would necessarily cushion a deterioration in the assets of the bank.

> gross capital to average assets ratio = $\dfrac{\text{gross capital}}{\text{average assets plus reserves}}$

Gross capital is defined as loan reserves plus debentures plus the stock-holders' common equity and preferred stock.

The gross capital of Aston Bank on 31 December 1988 was £8m. Its average assets, including reserves, were £102m. The bank's gross capital ratio was:

$$\frac{8,000,000}{102,000,000} = 7.8 \text{ per cent.}$$

The gross capital is very low and a sudden sharp deterioration in assets could wipe out the stockholders' equity in this company.

Primary capital to total assets

Primary capital is made up of stockholders' ordinary share, preferred stock, capital reserves and loan loss reserves.

The *primary capital to total assets ratio* shows how much of a deterioration in assets can be borne by the bank. It serves as a quick check to determine whether a bank is under-capitalised. The higher the ratio, the less risk for general creditors and vice versa.

> primary capital to total assets ratio = $\dfrac{\text{primary capital}}{\text{total assets}}$

The total assets of Ratcliffe Bank on 31 December 1988 were £5,808,000. On that day, stockholders' equity, capital reserves and loan loss reserves were £750,000, £820,000 and £1,000,000 respectively. Its primary capital to total assets ratio was:

$$\frac{750,000 + 820,000 + 1,000,000}{5,808,000} = 44.25 \text{ per cent.}$$

This indicates that the bank could bear a 44 per cent deterioration in its assets.

Primary capital to risk assets

The *primary capital to risk ratio* aims to identify the degree of comfort a bank has on account of its capital should there be a deterioration in the value of its risk assets. It is calculated as follows:

$$\text{primary capital to risk assets ratio} = \frac{\text{primary capital}}{\text{total assets} + \text{loan loss allowance} - \text{safe assets (cash, etc)}}$$

On 31 December 1988 Kane Bank had primary capital of £1,896,500. Its total assets were £19,632,500. It had cash of £286,100, government securities of £629,200 and a loan loss reserve of £362,100.

The primary capital ratio was:

$$\frac{1,896,500}{19,632,500 + 362,100 - 286,100 - 629,200} = 9.9 \text{ per cent.}$$

The primary capital is only 9.9 per cent and it cannot bear a loss in excess of 10 per cent of the risk assets.

Primary capital to non-performing loans

This ratio is examined by the analyst to determine whether primary capital is adequate to bear the loss that could result in non-performing loans becoming bad. Primary capital is, as in the previous ratio, defined as stockholders' common equity, preferred stock, capital reserves and loan loss reserves. The calculation is:

$$\text{primary capital to non-performing loans ratio} = \frac{\text{primary capital}}{\text{non-performing loans}}$$

The primary capital of John Bank was £20,800, whereas its non-performing loan was £18,900. The primary capital ratio is:

$$\frac{20,800}{18,900} = 110 \text{ per cent.}$$

The primary capital barely covers non-performing loans. Should a large write off be necessary, capital would be reduced enormously.

Primary capital to risk assets and guarantees

This ratio is an extension of the primary assets to risk assets ratio. It includes, in addition to risk assets, guarantees (standby letters of credit) which are a contingent liability. Thus, this ratio examines the total possible risks a bank has and the support that primary capital can give. The calculation is:

$$\text{primary capital to risk assets and guarantees ratio} = \frac{\text{primary capital}}{\text{risk assets and guarantees}}$$

The primary capital of Randolph Bank was £896,200 on 31 December 1988. Its risk assets on that day were £3,361,500 and it had outstanding guarantees of £236,100. Its primary capital to risk assets and guarantees ratio was:

$$\frac{896,200}{3,361,500 + 236,100} = 24.9 \text{ per cent.}$$

The bank's primary capital can support a deterioration of up to 25 per cent on the value of its risk assets and guarantees.

Secondary capital to total assets

The *secondary capital to total assets ratio*, if used along with the primary capital to total assets ratio, shows how much debt there is within the capital structure of a bank and how much comfort creditors can derive from this. Secondary capital is defined as primary capital, plus subordinated debt and preferred stock. The higher the ratio, the lower the risk for creditors. However, if the ratio is very high, the analyst should check whether the debt could be used by the bank to increase the primary capital so that the bank can grow. It is calculated as follows:

$$\text{secondary capital to total assets ratio} = \frac{\text{secondary capital}}{\text{total assets}}$$

The primary capital of Star Bank is £8,867,000. Its subordinated debt and preferred stock are £5,325,000 and £4,000,000 respectively. Its total assets are £54,900,000. Its secondary capital to total assets ratio is:

$$\frac{8{,}867{,}000 + 5{,}325{,}000 + 4{,}000{,}000}{54{,}900{,}000} = 33.1 \text{ per cent.}$$

The ratio is high. The bank's secondary capital can bear a fall in the value of assets by a third. The risk of other creditors is therefore low.

PART III
Limitations and conclusions

15. Limitations to the Use of Ratios

Ratio analysis provides an indication of a company's profitability liquidity, gearing and solvency. But ratios do not provide answers; they are merely a guide for management and others to the areas of a company's weakness and strengths.

However, ratio analysis is difficult and there are many limitations.

- many firms are very diversified, engaging in a number of different activities. This makes it difficult to develop a meaningful set of averages in order to compare performance;
- a ratio can be purposely distorted deliberately by a company to make it look better than it actually is. For example, a company could sell its debts at a discount for cash and as a result its collection ratio of debtors would be low, leading one to believe its efficiency to be greater than it actually is;
- in order to state whether a ratio is good or bad it must be intelligently interpreted. For example, a high current ratio may indicate, on the one hand, a liquidity position (which is positive) and, on the other excessive liquid cash (which is negative);
- it is difficult to use ratios to compare companies, because they very often follow different accounting principles. One company may value stock under the 'last in first out' principle, another may follow the 'first in first out' principle. Similarly, one company may depreciate assets under the straight-line method, while its competitor may use accelerated depreciation.

16.   Conclusion

Ratios are important tools of financial analysis. Ratio analysis used in a mechanical, unthinking manner can be misleading and useless and can lead to inaccurate conclusions. If it is used properly, it can provide powerful and valuable insights into a company's affairs.

It is important to remember that, prior to the ratios being computed, one must examine the financial statements and their accompanying notes and ensure that, in comparing performance and strengths, adjustments are made for variations from one year to the next. Some questions that should be asked and things that must be looked for are:

- do sales actually reflect economic reality?
- has any change in accounting principles taken place and, if so, what is its effect on the company's results and assets?
- have any debts been sold with recourse?
- does the company own a finance company that is unconsolidated and what would be the effect on the company if it were consolidated?
- are pension funds totally funded?
- are there any contingent liabilities that must be accounted for?
- is there any non-recurring income or expense?

It is also important to remember that a company may have some bad ratios and some good. It is incorrect to pass judgement on a company by looking at only one set of ratios. The ratios need to be seen altogether to obtain a true picture of how a company is performing.

Index of terms